G.A.T.E. Resource Center
718 Wallace Avenue
Wilkinsburg, PA 15221

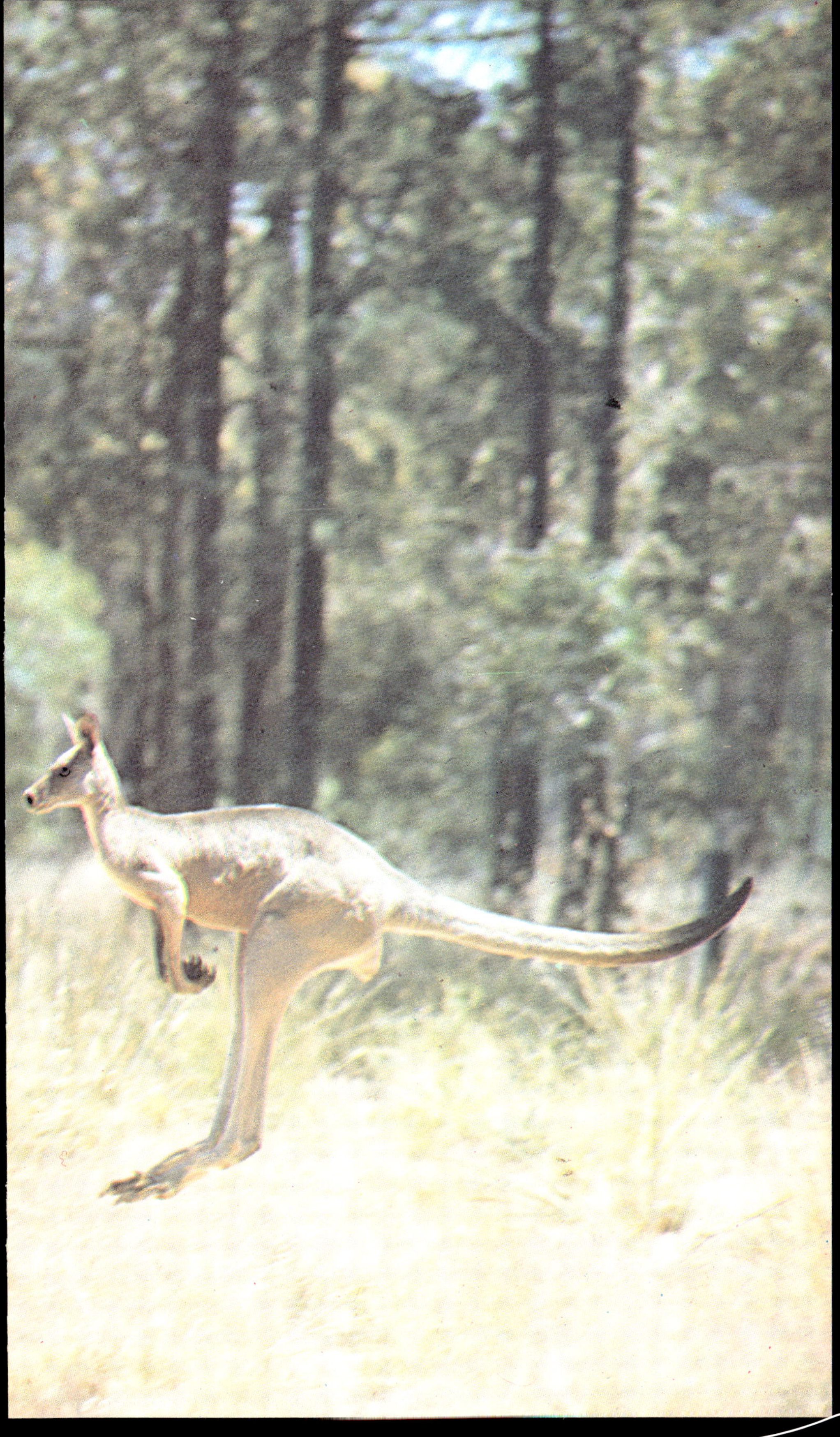

ANIMALS OF THE WORLD
Consultant Editor Sir Maurice Yonge CBE FRS

Kangaroos

Bernard Stonehouse

1 Curious Creatures	5
2 Kangaroos at Home	9
3 Kangaroos and Their Young	33
4 The Kangaroo Family	41
Glossary	54
Further Reading	56
Index	57

RAINTREE CHILDRENS BOOKS
Milwaukee • Toronto • Melbourne • London

U.S. edition text, copyright © 1977, Raintree Publishers Limited

First published in the United States of America by Raintree Publishers Limited, 1977.

Distributed to the Book Trade by the Two Continents Publishing Group, 30 East 42nd Street, New York, 10017.

All rights reserved. No part of this book may be reproduced or utilized in any form or by any means, electronic or mechanical, including photocopying, recording, or by any information storage and retrieval system, without permission in writing from the Publisher. Inquiries should be addressed to Raintree Publishers Limited, 205 West Highland Avenue, Milwaukee, Wisconsin 53203.

Library of Congress Number: 77-608272

International Standard Book Number: 0-8172-1079-2

2 3 4 5 6 7 8 9 0 81 80

Printed in England by Loxley Brothers Ltd.
Library bound in the United States of America.

First published in the United Kingdom by Wayland Publishers Ltd., 1977.
Copyright © 1977, Wayland Publishers Ltd.

Library of Congress Cataloging in Publication Data

Stonehouse, Bernard.
   Kangaroos.

   (Animals of the world)
   Bibliography: p. 56
   Includes index.
   SUMMARY: Describes the physical characteristics, habits, and natural environment of the large Red and Grey kangaroos and introduces other members of the kangaroo family.
   1. Kangaroos—Juvenile literature. [1. Kangaroos]
I. Title. II. Series.
QL737.M35S76   599'.2   77-60872
ISBN 0-8172-1079-2 lib. bdg.

Paperback edition ISBN 0-8467-0412-9

Introduction

The kangaroo is one of the world's most fascinating and unusual warm-blooded animals. At birth the baby is only 2.5 cm. (1 in.) long, but it immediately makes a three-minute journey to its mother's pouch. Fully grown, a male kangaroo is as tall as a man. No wonder the first explorers were puzzled by these strange jumping creatures that were so well suited to their hot, dry Australian home.

Filled with color photographs, this book introduces us to the various members of the kangaroo family and follows the lives of the large Red and Grey kangaroos in the forests and sandy deserts, where food and water are often scarce and survival depends upon the kangaroo's ability to travel fast across great distances.

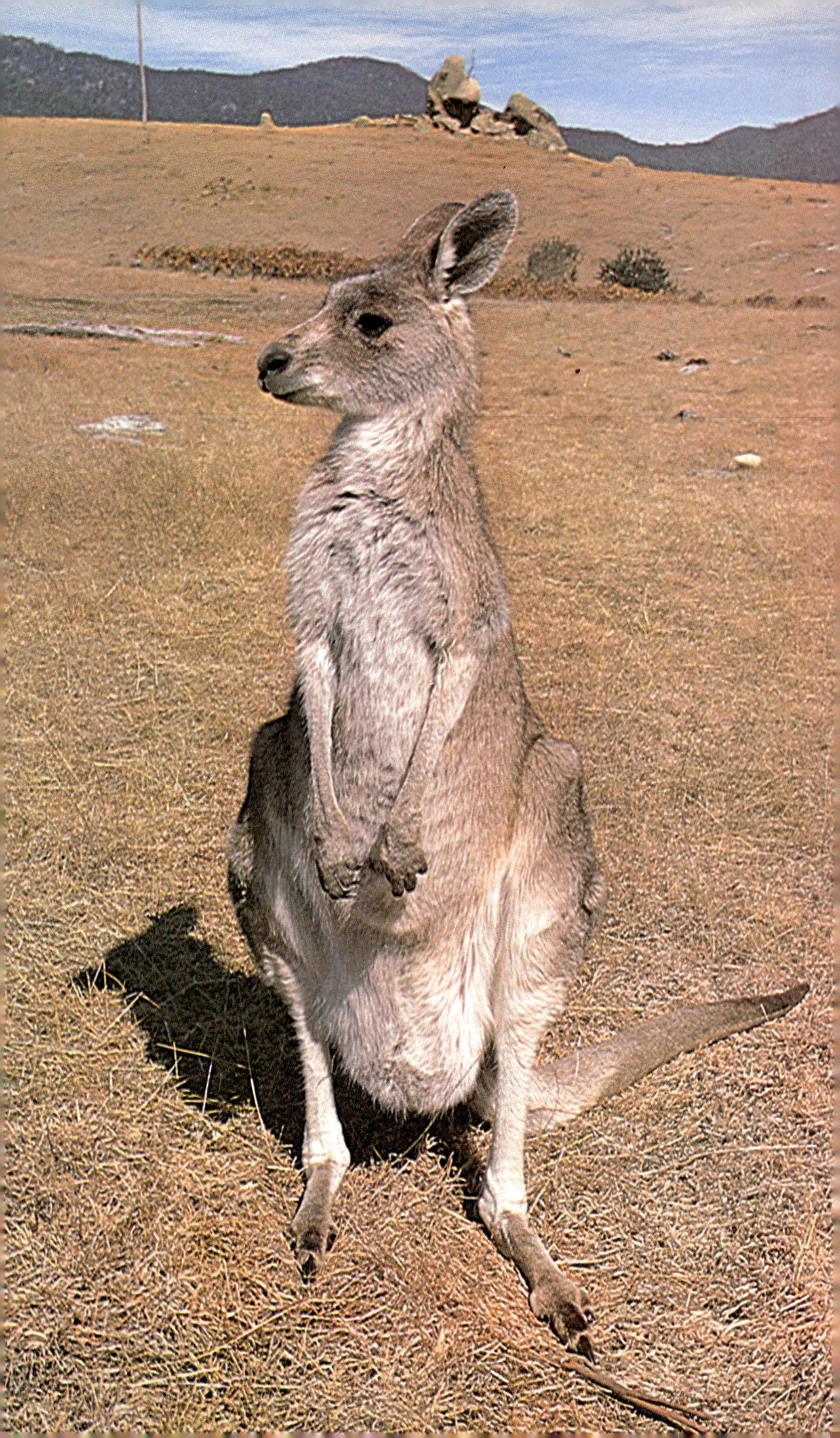

1
Curious Creatures

The first European explorers landed in Australia more than 350 years ago. There they found a kind of animal different from anything they had ever seen before. This animal was taller than a man. It had a doglike head with long, pointed ears. Its fur was reddish or mousy grey. Its shoulders were narrow, and its front legs were short, with paws like a monkey's. Its hind legs were enormous, with long, narrow feet. The tail, thin at the end with a thick, muscular base, was almost as long as the rest of the animal.

There were many of these strange animals, moving around in groups. When resting they squatted on their hind legs and tail, with body upright and front legs off the ground. Instead of running they hopped, taking great, flying leaps of 2.5 to 3 m. (8 to 10 ft.). They had little fear of humans, and often let the explorers get quite close. They never attacked and seemed content to sit eating grass and leaves.

Most curious of all, the females carried their young in a front pocket or pouch. Very small young nestled in the pocket, attached so firmly to the teats of the milk glands that they could not be removed without damage. Older ones climbed in and out of the pocket, leaving only their heads poking out. When danger threatened, they dived in headfirst and were carried to safety in leaps and bounds by the mother.

The native Australians called these animals "kangaroos." That has become the general name for the whole large family of long-tailed, bounding animals of Australia and New Guinea.

Today we call only the biggest ones kangaroos. There are two very similar species; one is the big Red kangaroo of central Australia. The other is the Grey or Forest kangaroo of eastern and southern Australia. Some of their smaller relations are known as wallabies (below), wallaroos, and pademelons.

In this book we are going to look at this curious creature and the life it leads. First we will visit the Red and Grey kangaroos at home in Australia.

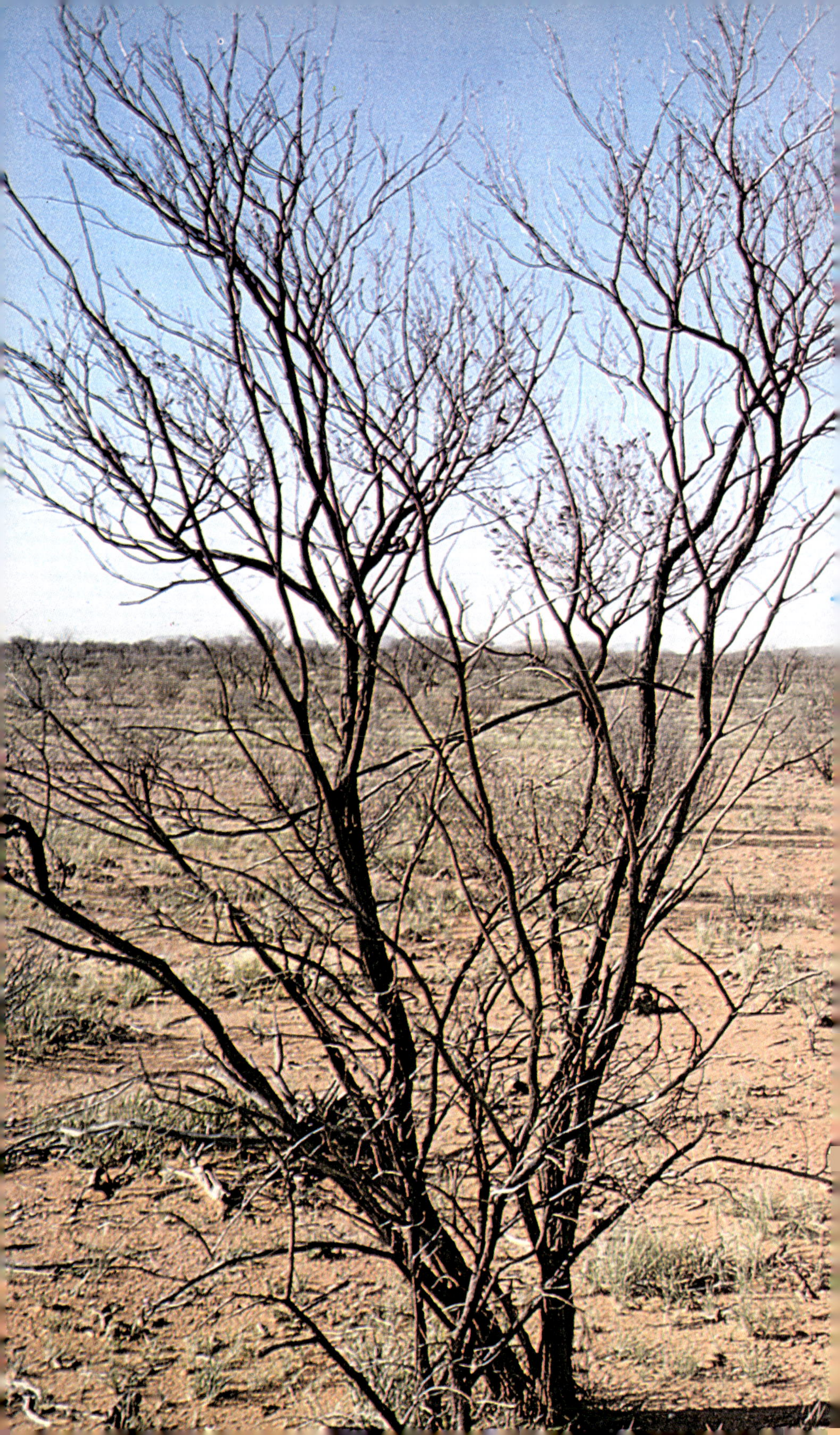

2
Kangaroos at Home

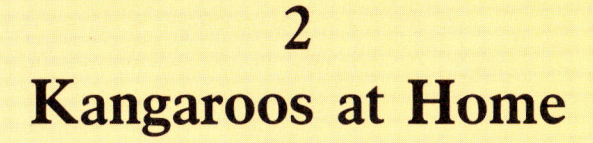

Australia is a huge continent. Its area is covered with a widely-varying landscape. Much of it is hot and dry, with sandy or stony deserts, parched grasslands, and large areas of thin forests and tree-dotted plains. In the wetter areas, especially in the east, north, and southwestern coastal regions, the forests are thicker and the grass grows more plentifully. Most of the big towns are near the coast. The drier areas are fenced off into huge farms, or sometimes left unfenced for cattle and sheep to range widely.

Kangaroos can be found all over Australia. They are equally at home on the driest plains of central Australia and in the densest forests of the coastal regions (right). The Red kangaroo ranges over some of the driest grasslands and semidesert areas. Grey kangaroos live mainly in the forest and woodland (below). Red kangaroos take their name from the males, which are usually reddish brown or tan. The females are often reddish grey or even silvery grey. Grey kangaroos are usually grey, but they can be reddish, too.

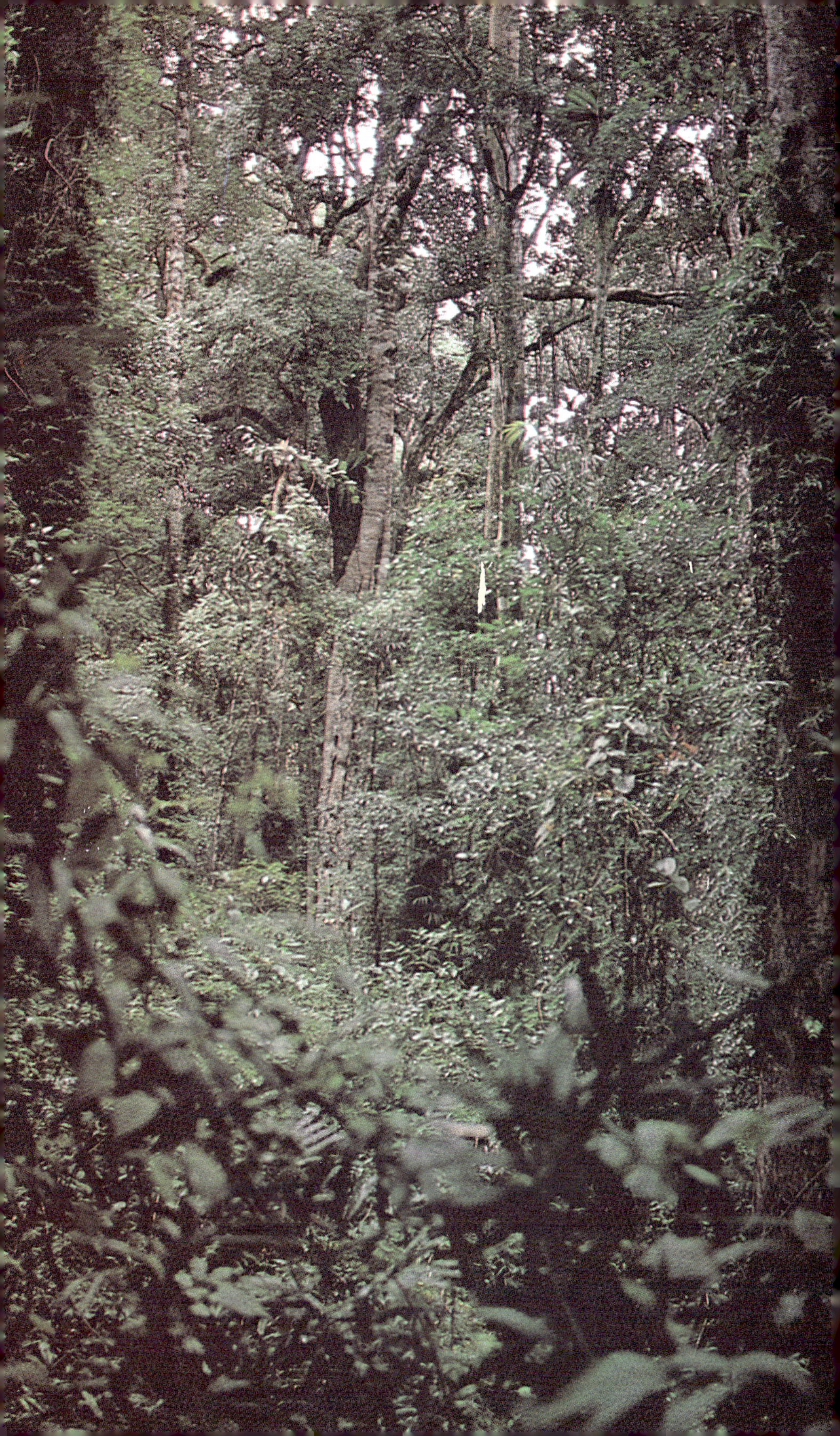

Large, fully grown males, such as these Reds, weigh an average of 50-60 kg. (110 to 130 lb.) and have been known to weigh up to 77 kg. (170 lb.). This is as much as a fully grown man. In their normal standing position they are about 1.5 m. tall (4-5 ft.), but when stretching up to sniff the air they may stand more than 2 m. tall (6.5 ft.). The big hind feet are up to 45 cm. long

(18 in.), and the tail is usually half the total length from tip of nose to tip of tail—up to 2.4 m. (8 ft.) in a fully grown animal. The fur is short and soft, reddish on the back but greyish white underneath. The legs and chin are white, with black-tipped paws and nose. It takes a male seven or eight years to reach full size.

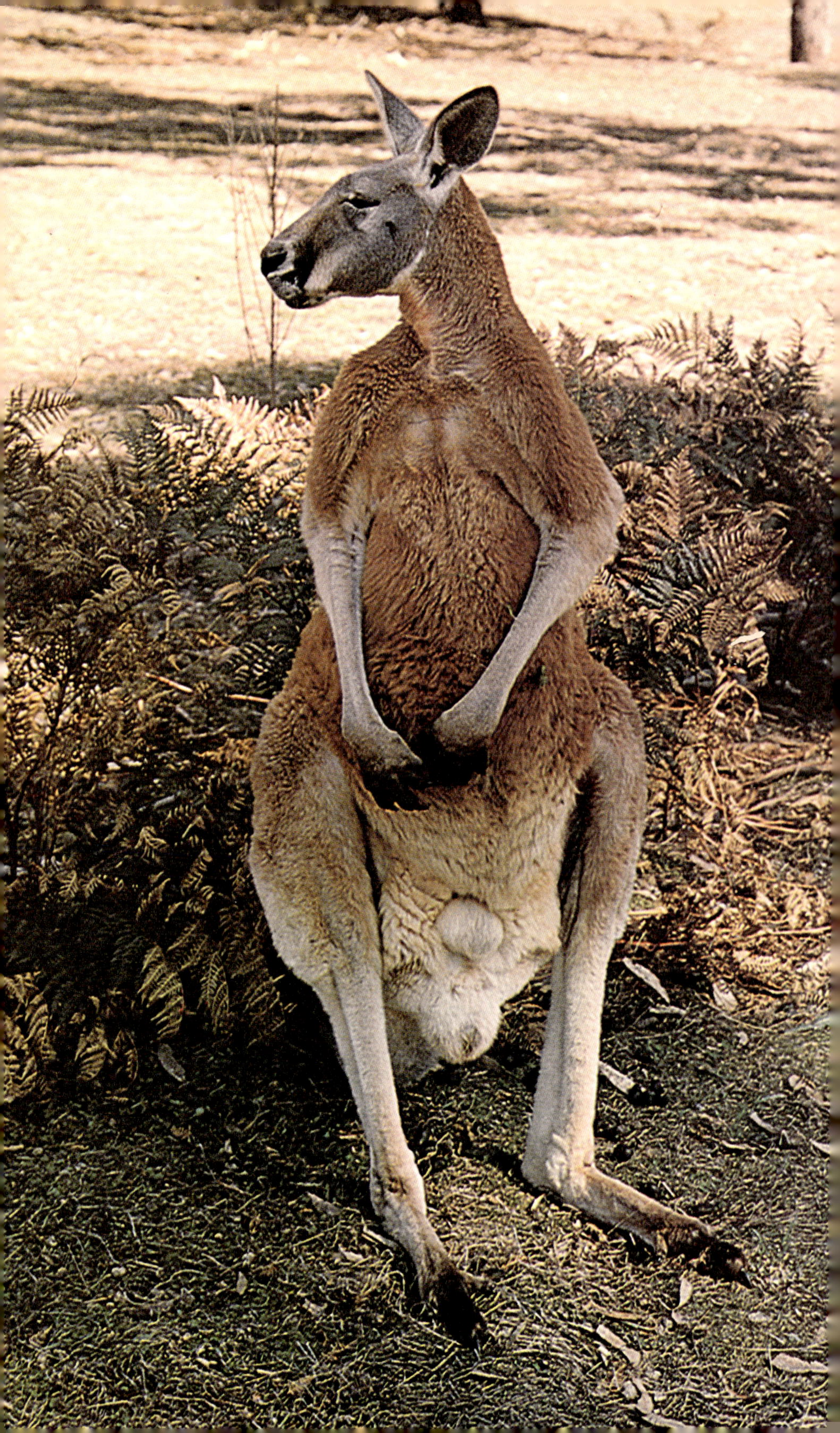

Female Red kangaroos are smaller than males. They seldom weigh more than 27 kg. (60 lb.) or stand more than 1.2 m. (4 ft.) tall. Where the males are red, the females are more silvery or bluish grey, with paler underside, legs, and chin. In some parts of central and western Australia, both males and females are red-brown. Young Red kangaroos are usually grey like their mothers throughout their first year. Then the males turn red. Whether male or female, young kangaroos are known as "joeys." Females reach their full size and weight in eight to ten years, but they may start breeding in their second year if they have had plenty of food.

Kangaroos are quiet, peaceable animals. They spend much of their time wandering in small groups in search of grazing and water. Though there are many thousands of them in Australia, they are nowhere very plentiful. In the really hot deserts, where food is poor and there is little water or shade, there may be few or no kangaroos at all. However, a freak shower of rain can change even the driest-looking desert into temporary grassland, and kangaroos are always on the move in search of new grass to eat and water to drink.

Kangaroos can survive for several days without food, water, and shade. But they like a regular supply of water and prefer feeding where streams or water holes provide an evening drink. They also like to feed where there are enough trees or shrubs to give shade during the heat of the day. So they are more plentiful in bush and grassland areas and densest of all in rich, well-watered grasslands where there are also forests. These Red kangaroos have found a pleasant patch of woodland in which to feed. Where conditions are right for them, they move very little, returning to the same shade and drinking places each day. After several months without rain, when food and water are becoming scarce, they may have to travel long distances to find the supplies they need to stay alive.

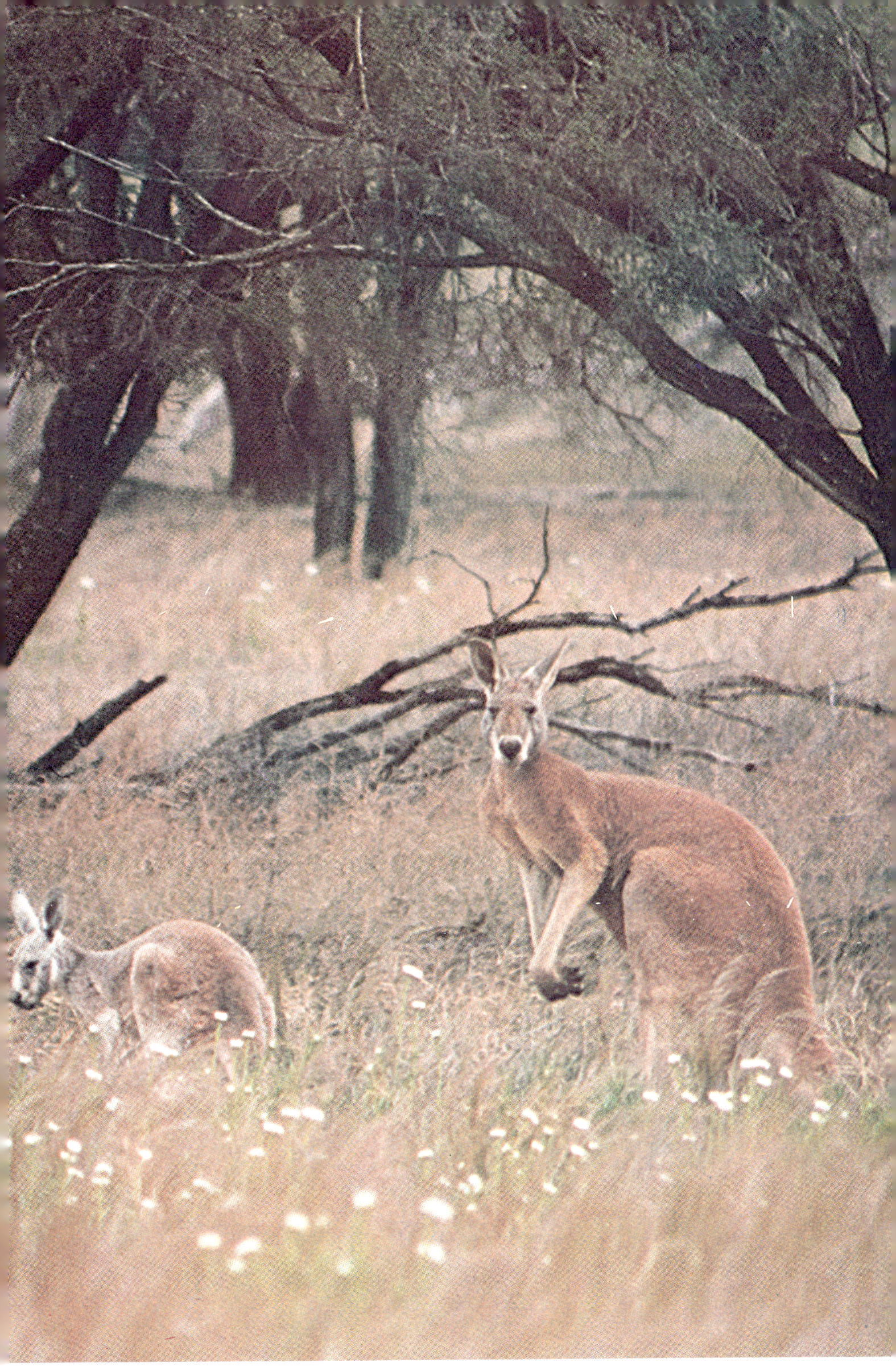

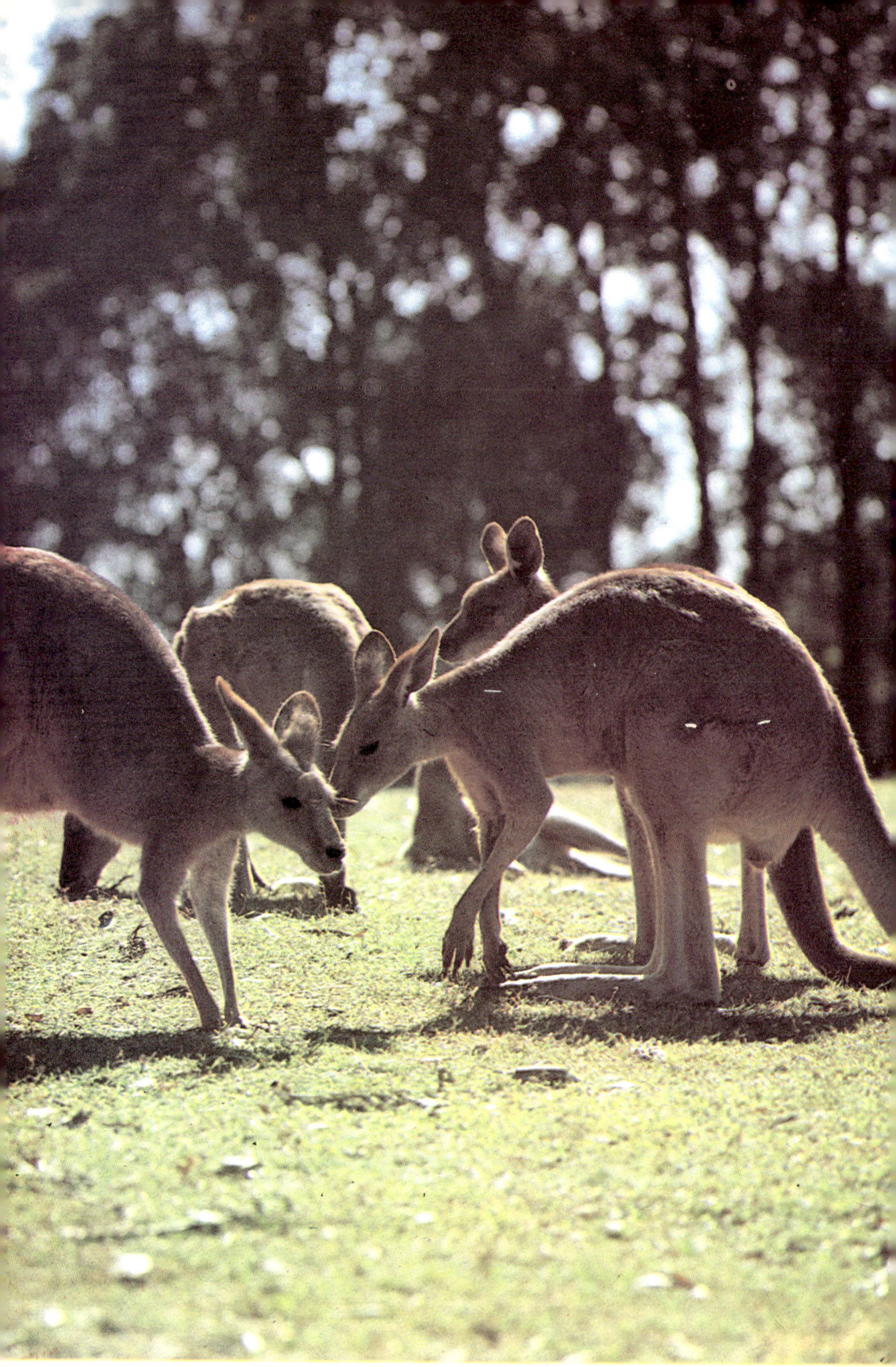

A group of kangaroos is known as a "mob." A mob usually includes a large mature male, two or three females with joeys in the pouch or running behind them, and two or three young males, which join or leave from time to time. They feed quietly, often pausing to look around or sniff the air, moving off if they are approached by people or dogs. A joey remains with its own mother, running to her if danger threatens. These are probably family groups, which the large males lead for several months or even years.

Where grazing is good, a number of family mobs may gather together and feed side by side without fighting. When more than a dozen Red kangaroos are seen together, they are usually made up of two or more family parties. Where feeding is especially lush, several hundred may gather. When the grass is eaten and new grazing must be sought, the large groups break up again into small family parties.

Female kangaroos hardly ever fight. Males sometimes square up to each other and box or grapple like wrestlers in a ring. Sometimes they may fight more fiercely, perhaps when one of the females is in heat and ready to mate. They claw each other with their front paws and, settling back on their tails, lash out with their powerful hind legs, bruising or even ripping open their opponent.

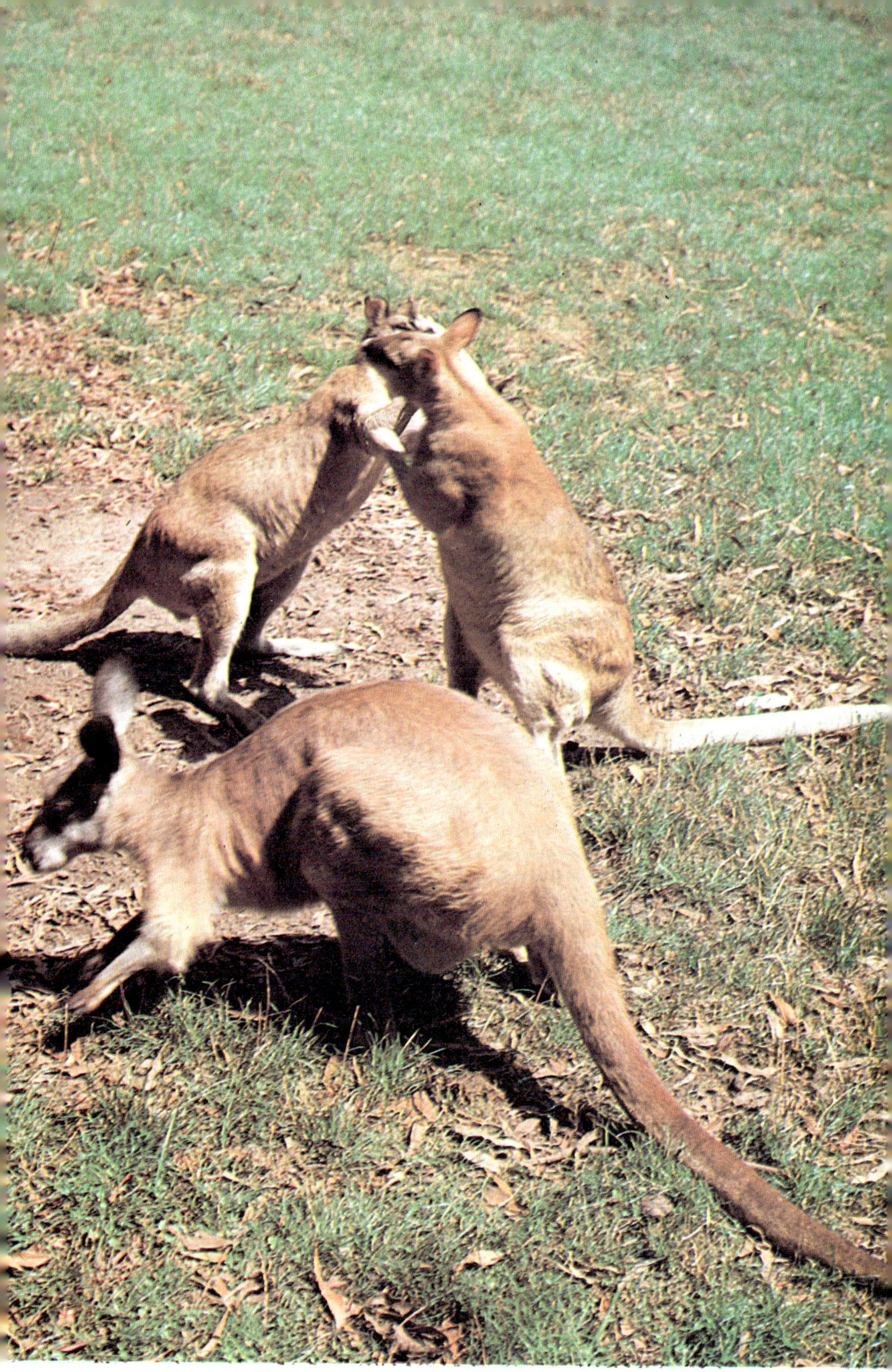

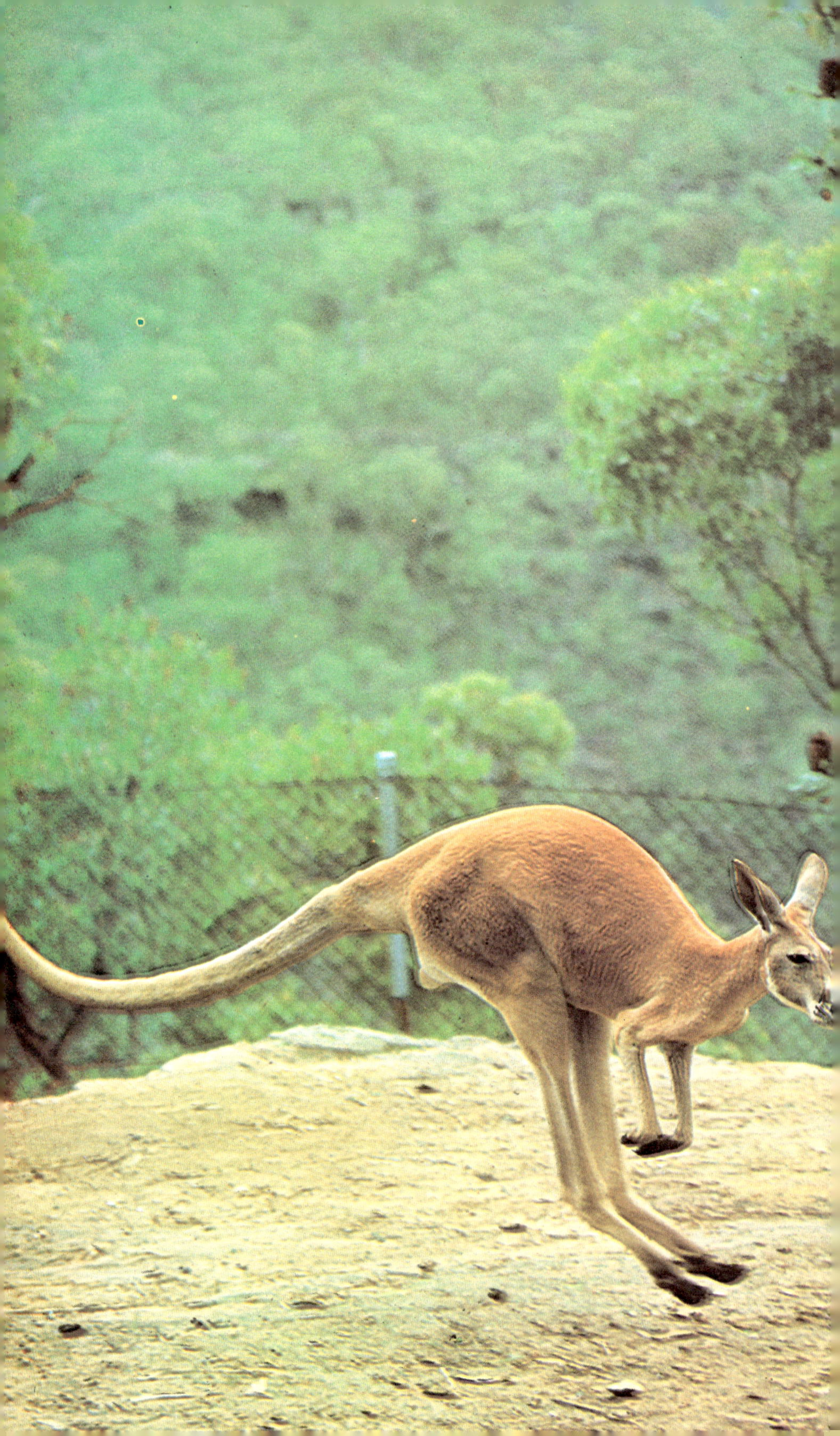

When grazing and moving slowly from place to place, kangaroos go down on all fours, often using the tail as an extra prop. When they are in a hurry, only the hind limbs are used, carrying the animal forward in graceful bounds. The tail stretches out behind, helping the kangaroo keep its balance. At low speeds leaps of 1.5-2 m. (4-6 ft.) are usual. At high speeds kangaroos can cover 6 m. (20 ft.) or more in a single bound, clearing 2 m. (6 ft.) fences as they go. A fast-moving Red kangaroo travels at about 55 km. (35 mi.) per hour but soon tires at that speed; up to 15 km. (9-10 mi.) per hour is a good average speed. The lightweight females, called "blue fliers," tend to travel faster than the heavier males.

Kangaroos have large ears, which are constantly twitching and turning when the animals are alert; they probably have good hearing. They also seem to have a sharp sense of smell. Good eyesight lets them see movement a long way off. They make little noise; mothers and young squeak and cluck to each other, and males grunt or cough when they threaten each other or fight. An alarmed kangaroo thumps the ground hard with his hind legs, especially when leaping away from danger. This acts as an alarm signal to other kangaroos standing by. They take off immediately, without pausing to see where the danger lies.

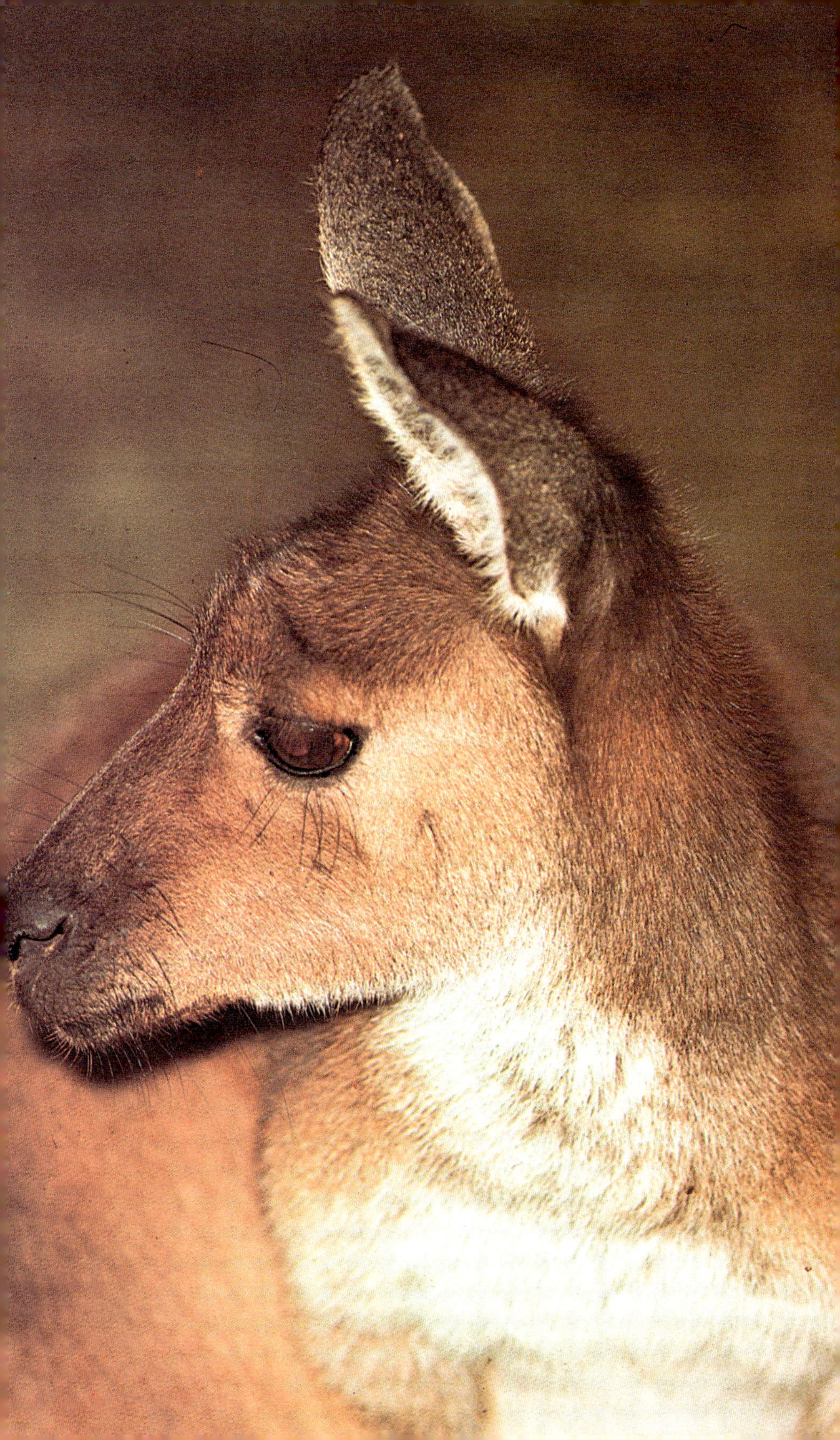

When food is plentiful, kangaroos, sheep, and cattle grazing side by side like to eat different plants. Kangaroos usually prefer grass, while cattle and sheep will also browse on other plants.

When food is scarce, all the animals eat what they can get. Because a kangaroo eats about as much as a sheep, farmers often feel that they cannot afford to have too many kangaroos on their thin pastures. They try to keep the animals' numbers down by shooting them. Kangaroos also drink at farm water holes, however, and a man-made water hole often allows them to live in an area where they would otherwise be unable to survive.

In very hot weather kangaroos feed mostly in the mornings, even before sunrise, and late at night when the sun is down and the ground has cooled. These are the times of day when plants contain most moisture. When the animals eat they take in water as well as food. This helps to reduce their need for drinking. During the heat of the day kangaroos, like this Grey, often seek the shade of trees and shrubs. They form "nests," or hollows in the dust, and sometimes throw sand over themselves. This helps them to keep cool. Flies are a great bother to them at these times, biting their lips, eyelids and ears and buzzing constantly about them.

Sometimes in the hot weather they wander restlessly at night in search of food or water. Man-made fences designed to keep in sheep do not stop kangaroos, which scramble through or leap over them. In cool weather kangaroos feed much more during the day, spending more of their nights at rest.

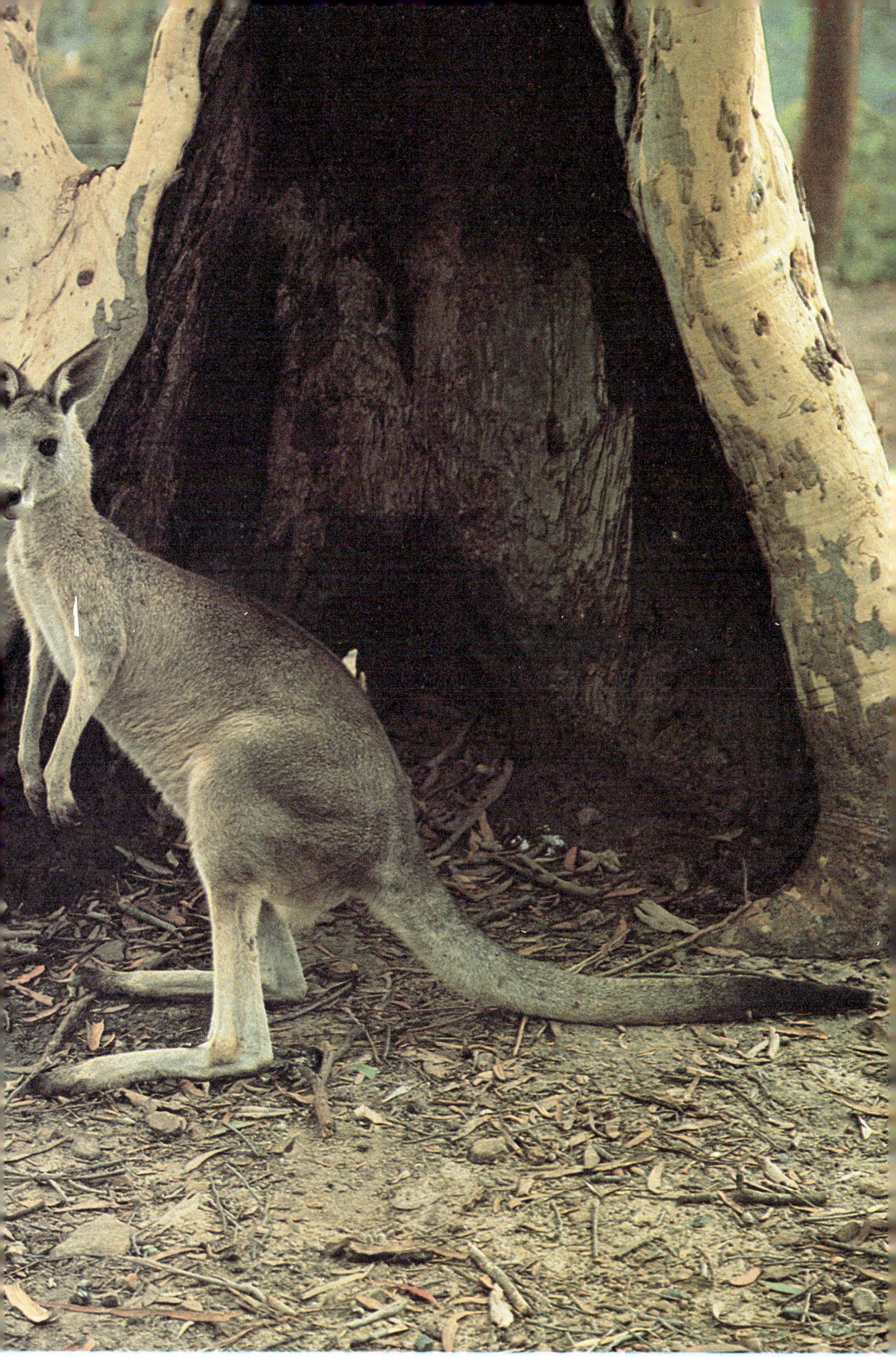

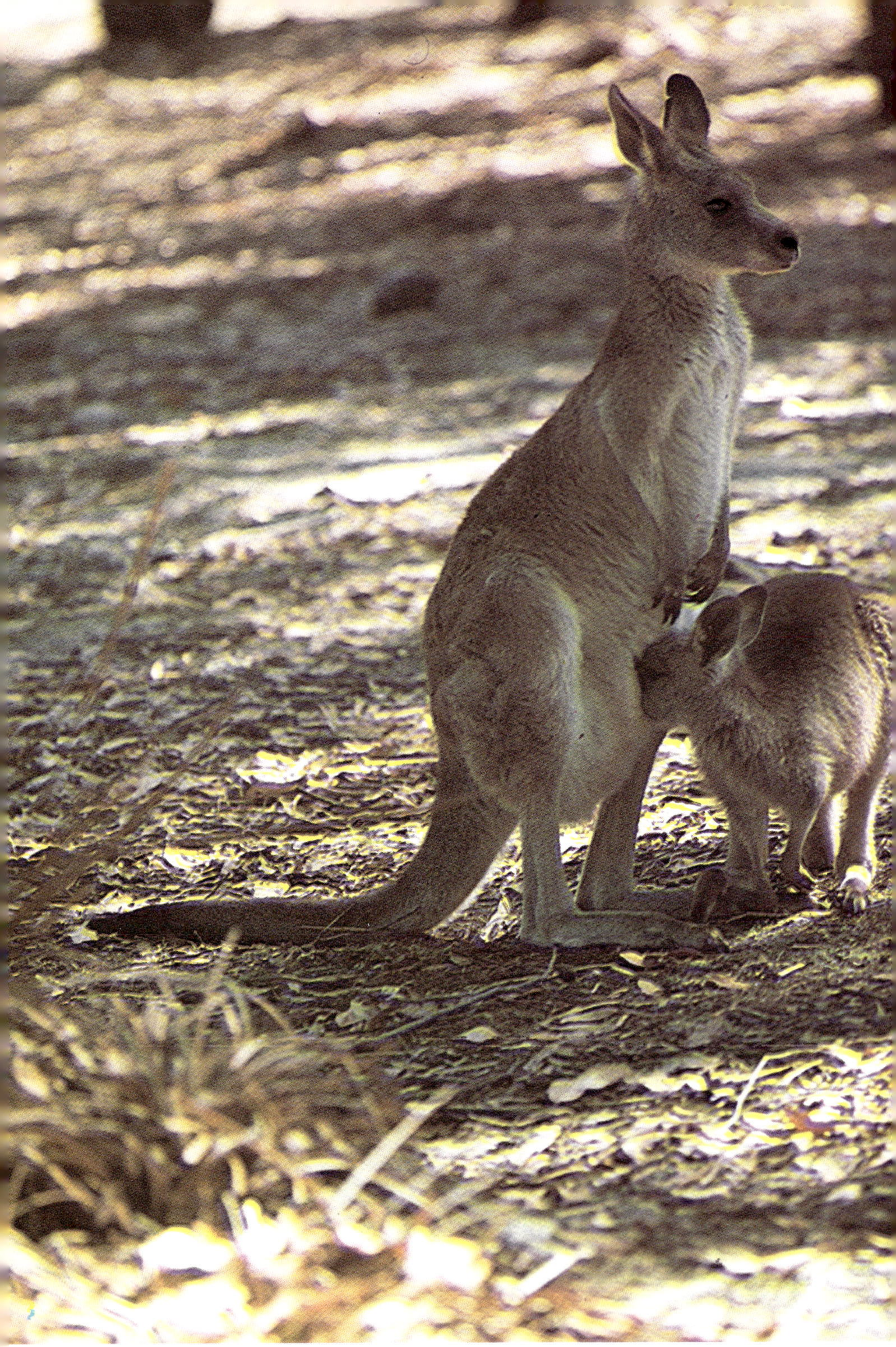

3
Kangaroos and Their Young

Red kangaroos can breed at any time of year. They breed most successfully when rain has been plentiful and the grass is growing well. Then the mothers have plenty of food, the joeys have all the milk they need, and many survive. In times of drought the mothers go hungry, and they stop making milk. Then many joeys die of starvation. Grey kangaroos, usually living where there is more food and water, mate and give birth in spring and early summer.

In Red kangaroos the gestation period is only about five weeks. When the baby kangaroo is born it is only about 2.5 cm. (1 in.) long. It weighs about 1 g. ($\frac{1}{28}$ oz.).

It is pink and hairless, with transparent skin. Its head is fairly big, but it has a very small body, hind quarters, and tail. It looks far too weak to be released into the world, and indeed has to be protected in the safety of the pouch for many weeks to come.

To reach that safety it must crawl from the birth canal opening to the pouch. It does this by moving its arms one after the other and wriggling its head and body from side to side. It reaches the pouch in about three minutes. Once inside, the joey attaches itself to one of the four teats there. Its jaw muscles and tongue are strong enough to hold it in place, and it remains fixed to the teat for several weeks. The mother's rich milk is injected rather than sucked into the joey's mouth.

The baby joey grows quickly. After eight to twelve weeks it lets go of its mother's teat and pokes its head out of her pouch to look around at the world outside. After fifteen or sixteen weeks it tumbles out of the pouch. But it is always ready to dive back again at the slightest sign of danger. After six to eight months, if food has been plentiful, it may almost be able to look after itself. It nibbles grass and leaves and only feeds from its mother once in a while. A joey that has reached this stage stands a good chance of growing into an adult, though it must still be wary of enemies. When dogs, dingoes, foxes, or people with guns are about, the young must stay as much as possible in the safety of the mob.

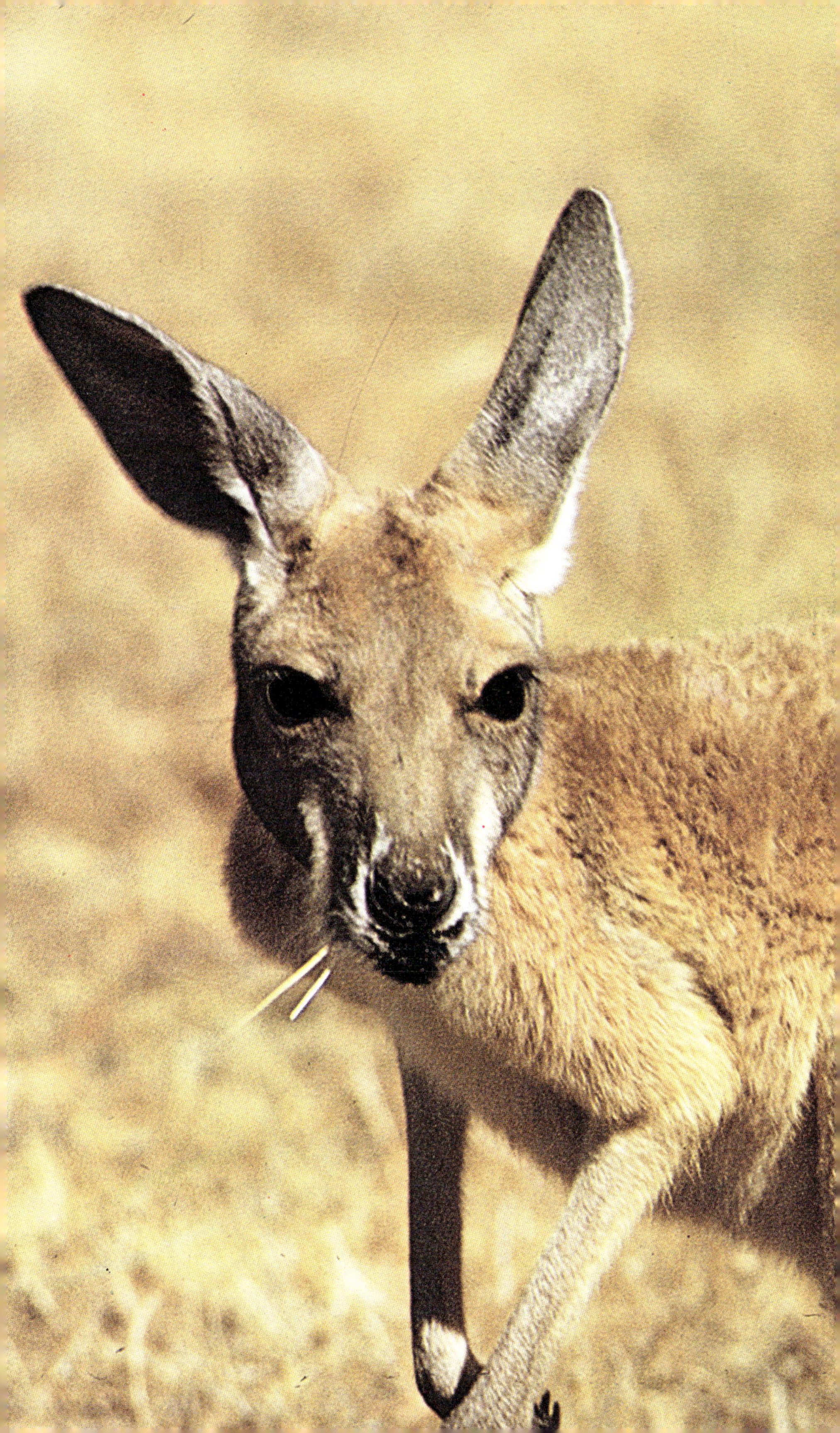

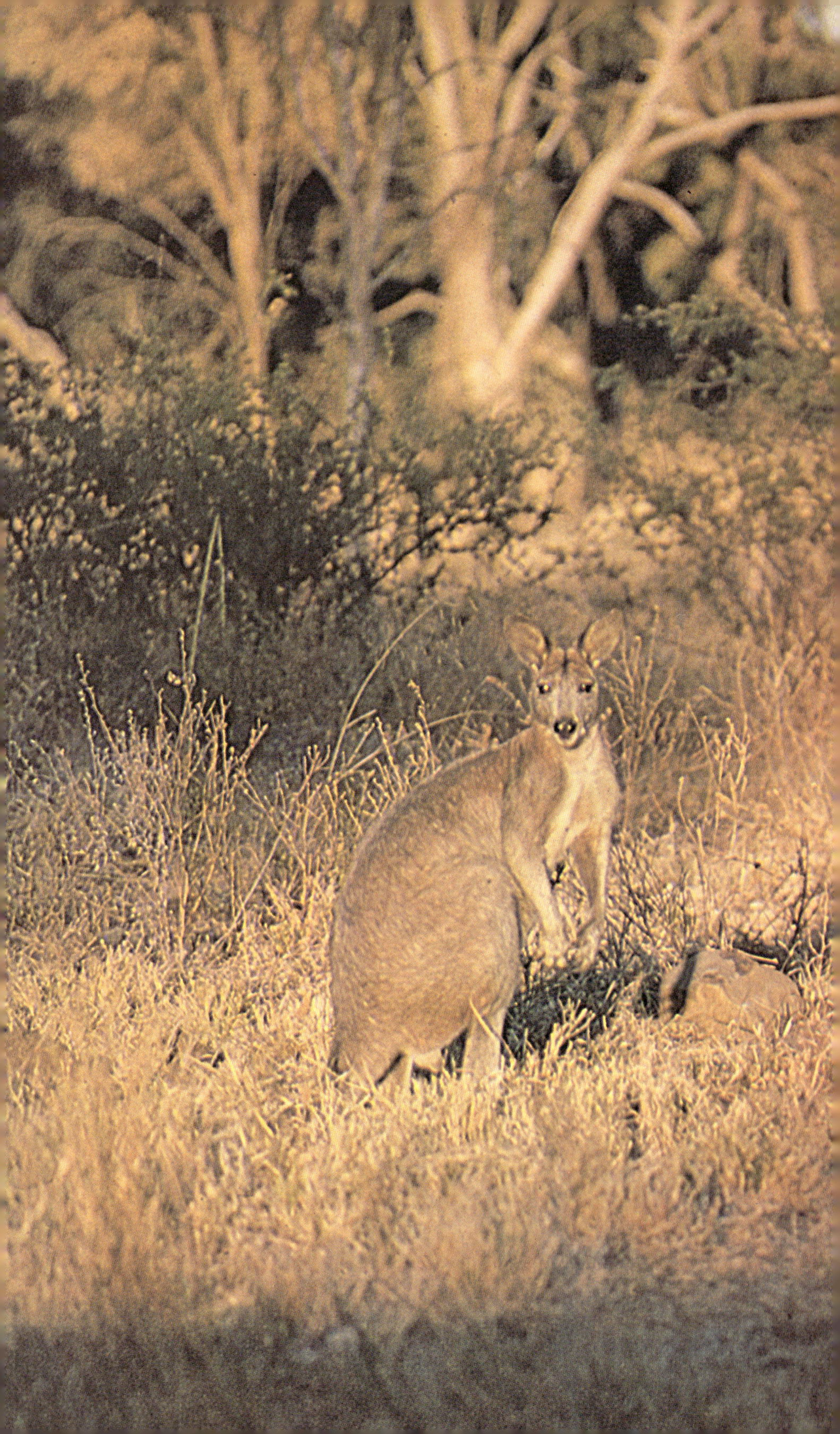

4
The Kangaroo Family

We are now going to look at other members of the kangaroo family, starting with wallabies. Wallabies are small kangaroos. They weigh from 2 to about 22 kg. (4-50 lb.). There are many different kinds. Most of them live in the damper, wooded areas of Australia and New Guinea. Several species can be seen in zoos, where they survive well. Some that have escaped from zoos, or that have been freed on purpose, live well enough in European countries. They even breed successfully each year. This is the Pretty-faced or Whip-tailed wallaby, which lives on open hillsides and woodlands in eastern Australia.

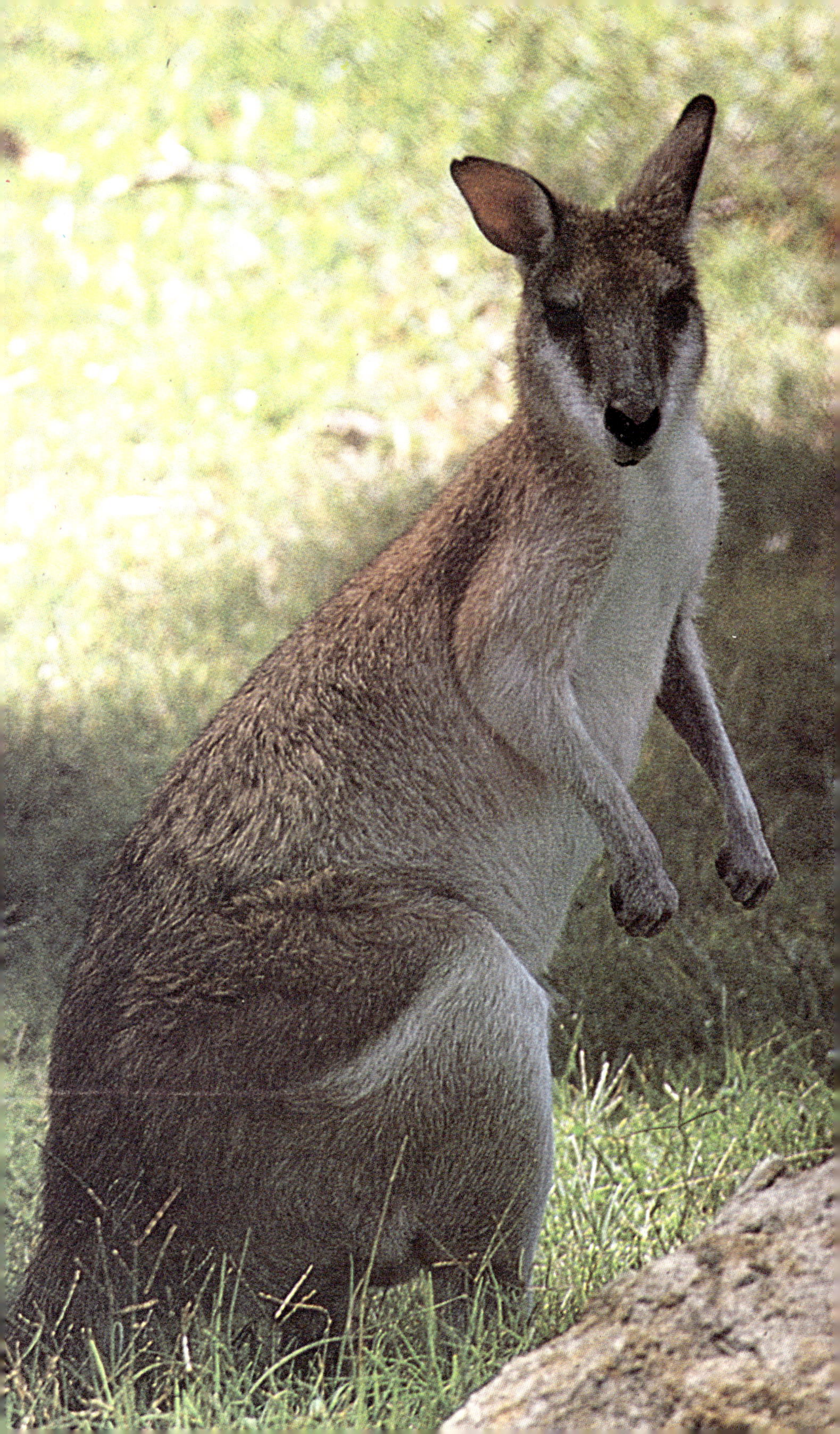

Hare wallabies are the size of a large rabbit or hare and tend to live in open nests or "forms," like hares. Once plentiful and widespread, they have been driven away from many parts of their former range by hunting and farming. This species, the Banded hare wallaby (below), was once common in Western Australia but now survives only on offshore islands.

Pademelons are small wallabies that live rather like rabbits in grassland and forest. Their "burrows" are tunnels in long grass, where they hide from dingoes, foxes, and other predators, including humans. This is the Red-legged pademelon of northeastern Queensland (above). It is a plump little wallaby, which both the aboriginals and the early white settlers of Australia hunted for food.

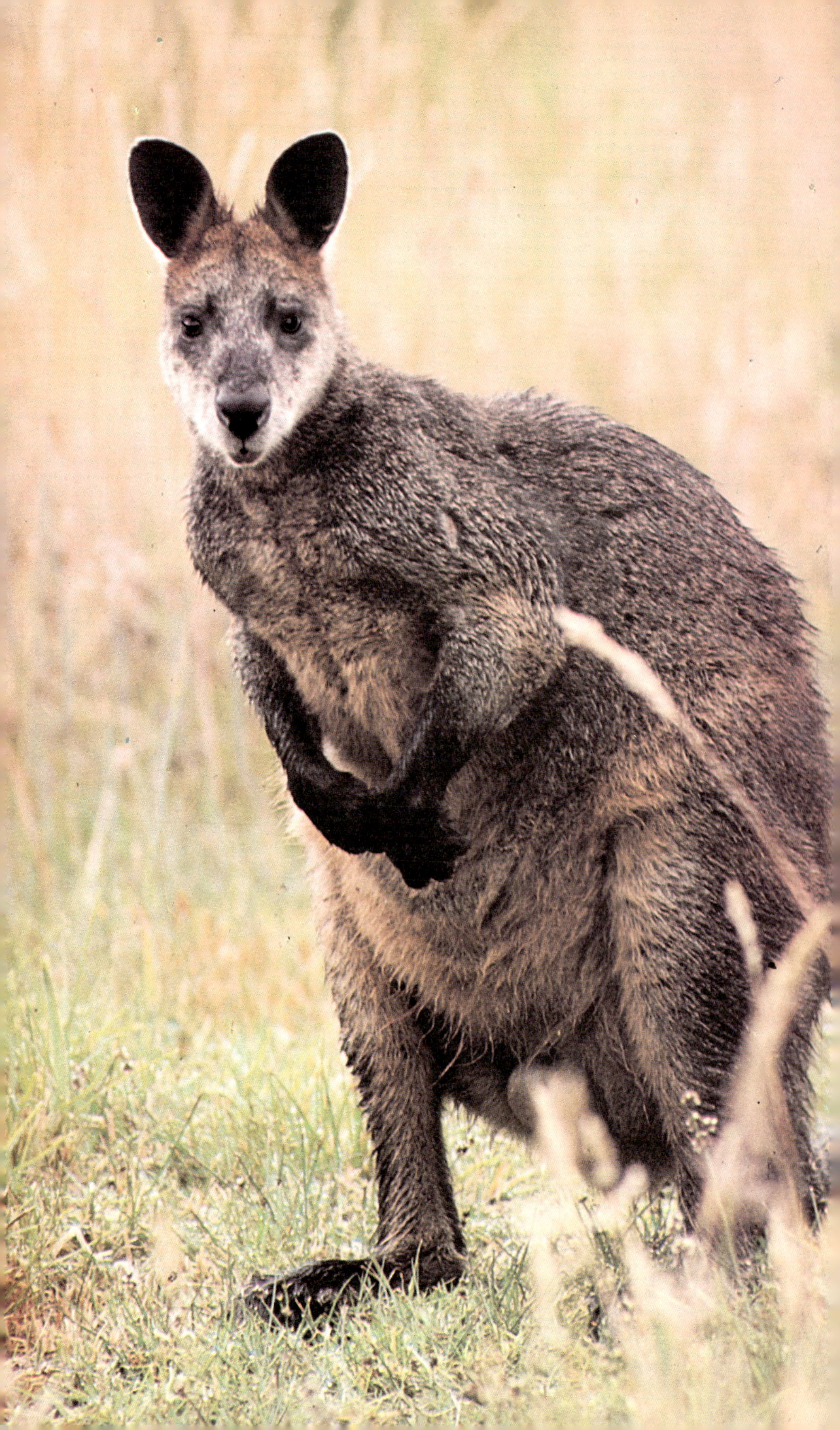

The Swamp or Black-tailed wallaby is plentiful in Victoria, New South Wales, and Queensland. It prefers damp, heavily wooded, or even marshy country, where dense ferns and long grass provide plenty of cover. It is often found in deep, tree-lined gullies among the eastern mountains. This choice of habitat has helped it to survive the many changes brought about in Australia since farming began. The kangaroos and wallabies living on the plains have been driven away by sheep and crop-production. But the Swamp wallabies of the hills and gullies have been left much more to themselves.

Rat kangaroos form a small group slightly apart from the true kangaroos and wallabies. Weighing only 0.5 to 3 kg. (1-6 lb.), they live mostly in grassland and feed mainly on roots and seeds. One species, the boodie, lives in burrows that it scratches for itself in damp earth. Another species, the musky, feeds mainly on earthworms and insects. It can also eat grass, leaves, and berries when animal foods are scarce. The

Potoroo or Long-nosed rat kangaroo, shown below, was once common throughout eastern Australia. Now hunting and the destruction of its habitat restricts it mainly to Tasmania.

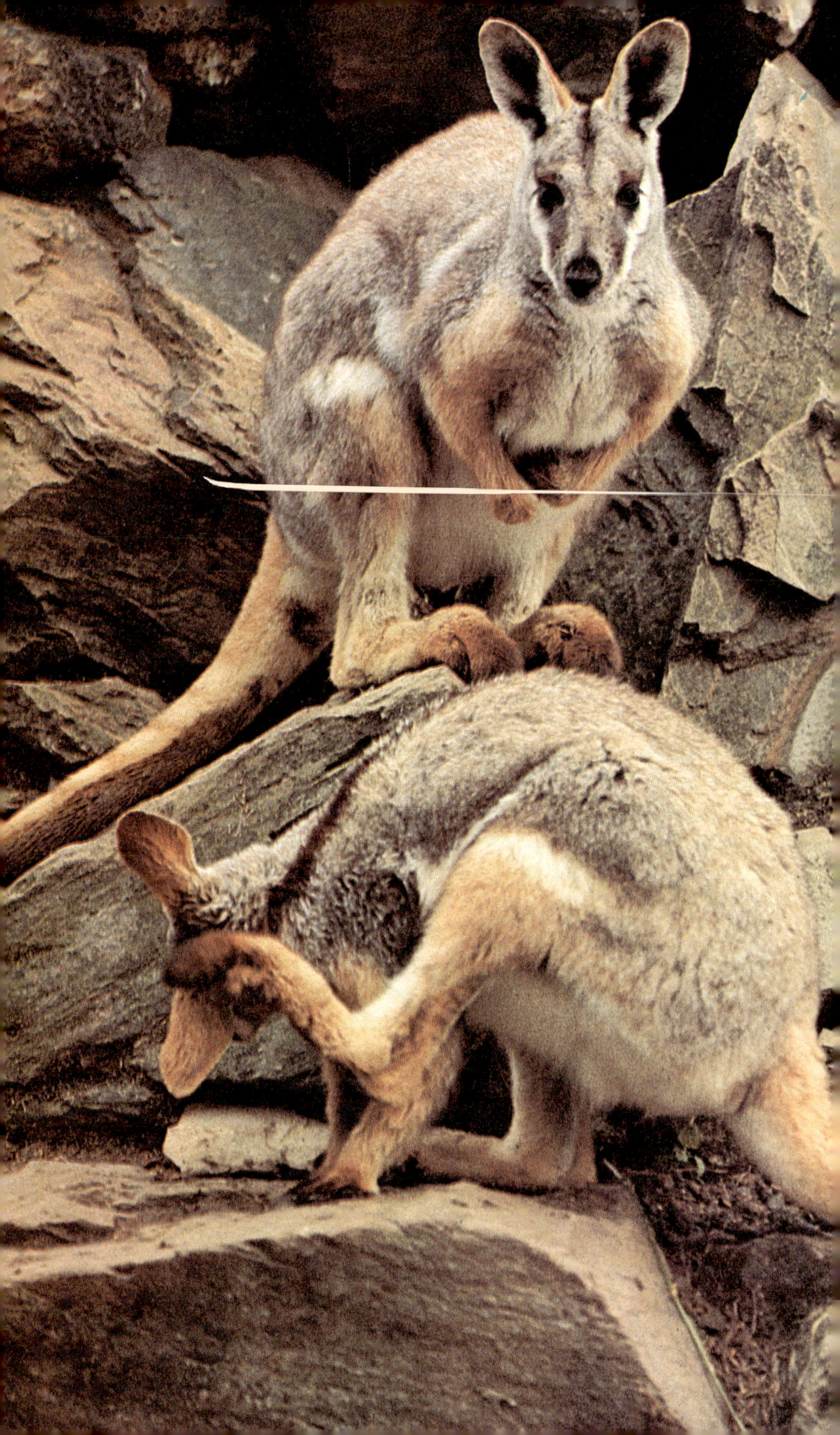

Rock wallabies have the short fore limbs and long hind limbs of kangaroos, but the hind feet are flexible and padded. These wallabies live in areas of broken, craggy rock and are very good at climbing and scrambling. They jump fearlessly over deep chasms and leap about among the high branches of tall trees. The Ring-tailed rock wallaby, shown here, is one of the showiest of all the marsupials. Hunters prize its thick, rich fur, but its out-of-the-way habitat has helped to save it from extinction.

Perhaps the strangest of all kangaroos are the Tree kangaroos of Australia and New Guinea. Their fore limbs and hind limbs are almost equal in length. The hind toes are short and flexible, with ribbed soles and curved claws. These help them to hold on to the branches of the trees where they live. They are found high above the ground in dense tropical forest, climbing, perching, and leaping from tree to tree with all the ease of ground-living kangaroos. The long tail with its tufted tip helps them to keep their balance. This is Lumholtz's tree kangaroo of northern Queensland.

So you see that the kangaroo family is a large and varied one. The next time you see a kangaroo in a zoo, imagine yourself as one of the early explorers of Australia, seeing it for the first time. Compared to the other animals, what a curious creature it is.

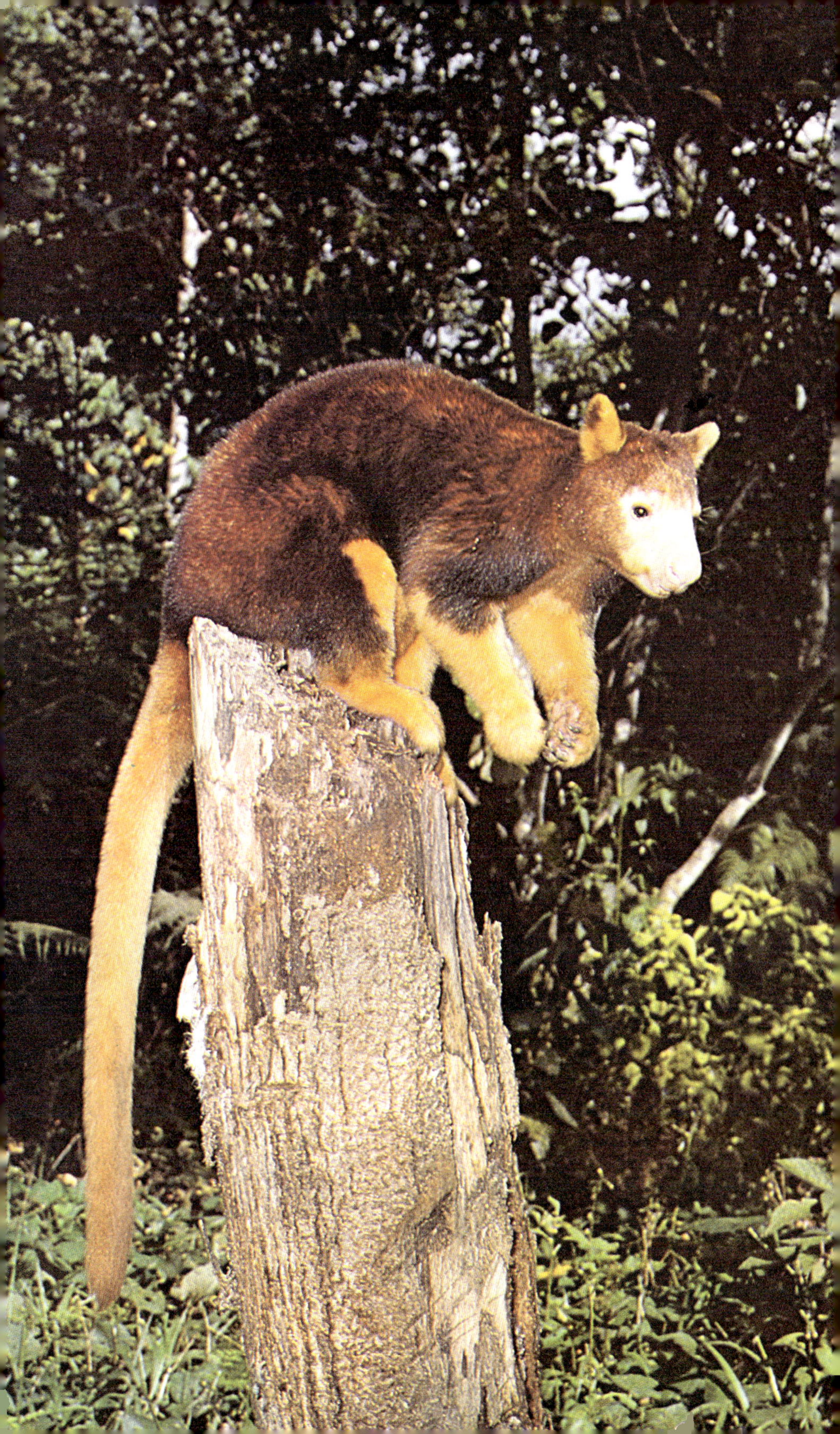

Glossary

BLUE FLIER A female Red kangaroo; so called because of the shade of its fur and the speed at which it travels.

DINGO Wild dog living in Australia.

GESTATION PERIOD The time between mating and birth, when the young animal is growing inside its mother.

GULLY A deep channel in a rock carved out by water.

HABITAT The living area and surroundings of an animal.

JOEY A young kangaroo of any age.

KANGAROO A member of the family *Macropodidae*; on its own, the name usually applies only to the large Red and Grey kangaroos, but it can also include the wallabies, tree kangaroos, etc.

MAMMAL A member of the class *Mammalia*: animals that are warm-blooded, have hair, usually produce their young alive, and always feed their young on milk from special glands.

MAMMARY GLANDS Special glands, usually on the chest or abdomen, in which mammals produce milk for their young.

MARSUPIAL A mammal that produces its young after a fairly short gestation period and usually rears them in a pouch or pocket of skin on the abdomen.

MOB A group of kangaroos.

PADEMELON A small wallaby of the genus *Thylogale*; there are several species.

SAVANNAH Sparse grassland dotted with shrubs and bushes.

TEATS The nipples, or openings of the mammary glands, through which young mammals suck milk.

WALLABY A small species of kangaroo.

WALLAROO A species of kangaroo halfway in size between the large Red and Grey kangaroos and the wallabies; also called a Euro.

YEARLING A young animal over one, but not yet two years old.

Further Reading

Burton, Maurice, and Burton, Robert, editors. *The New International Wildlife Encyclopedia.* 21 vols. Milwaukee: Purnell Reference Books, 1980.

Coerr, Eleanor. *Biography of a Kangaroo.* New York: G. P. Putnam's Sons, 1976.

Crowcroft, Peter. *Australian Marsupials.* McGraw-Hill Book Company, 1972.

Hurd, Edith. *The Mother Kangaroo.* Waltham, Mass.: Little, Brown & Company, 1976.

Jenkins, Marie M. *Kangaroos, Opossums, and Other Marsupials.* New York: Holiday House, 1975.

Lauber, Patricia. *Surprising Kangaroos and Other Pouched Mammals.* Westminster, Md.: Random House, 1965.

ACKNOWLEDGMENTS

The author and publisher would like to thank the following for their permission to reproduce copyright illustrations on the pages mentioned: Ardea London, jacket front, 12, 19, 23, 32, 49 (Hans & Judy Beste), endpaper (W. R. Taylor); Natural Science Photos, 4, 11, 13, 14, 16, 17, 29, 34, 39, 40-41, 43 (C. A. Walker), 8-9 (J. A. Grant); N.H.P.A. 6, 7, 10, 20, 24-25, 27, 28, 31, 36, 50-51 (Douglas Baglin), 22 (L. Hugh Newman), 37 (M. Morcombe); Bruce Coleman, jacket front, 44 (V. Serventy), 45 (Graham Pizzey), 46 (J. R. Brownlie); Frank Lane, 35 (J. E. R. Finch), 48 (Frank W. Lane), 53 (Len Robinson).

Index

Australia, 7, 9, 10, 42, 47, 52
Baby kangaroos, 34-38
Breeding, 15, 33-34
Cattle, 9, 28

Danger, 6, 26
Deserts, 9, 10, 16, 17
Dingoes, 38, 45
Drinking, 16, 17, 18, 21, 29, 30
Drought, 17, 18, 33

Ears, 26
Enemies, 38
Eyesight, 26

Farming, 9, 29, 44, 47
Fighting, 22
Flies, 30
Forests, 9, 10, 18, 51, 52
Foxes, 38, 45
Fur, 13, 51

Grassland, 9, 10, 18
Grazing, 16, 17, 18, 21, 25, 28, 29, 30, 38
Grey kangaroos, 10, 33

Hare wallabies, 44
Heat, 30
Height, 12, 15
Hopping, 5, 25
Hunting, 44, 45, 51

Joeys, 6, 15, 21, 33, 35, 36, 38

Legs, 12, 13, 25, 51, 52

Mobs, 21, 38

Nests, 30
New Guinea, 6, 42, 52
New South Wales, 47
Noises, 26

Pademelons, 7, 45
Paws, 13
Potoroo, 49
Pouch, 6, 36, 38
Pretty-faced wallaby (Whip-tailed wallaby), 42

Queensland, 45

Rat kangaroos, 48, 49
Red kangaroos, 10, 12, 15, 21, 25, 33
Rock wallabies, 51

Savannah, 9
Sheep, 9, 28
Speed, 25
Swamp wallaby (Black-tailed wallaby), 47

Tail, 12, 25
Tasmania, 49
Teat, 6, 37
Tree kangaroos, 52

Victoria, 47

Wallabies, 7, 42, 44, 47, 51
Wallaroos, 7
Weight, 12, 15
Western Australia, 44

57

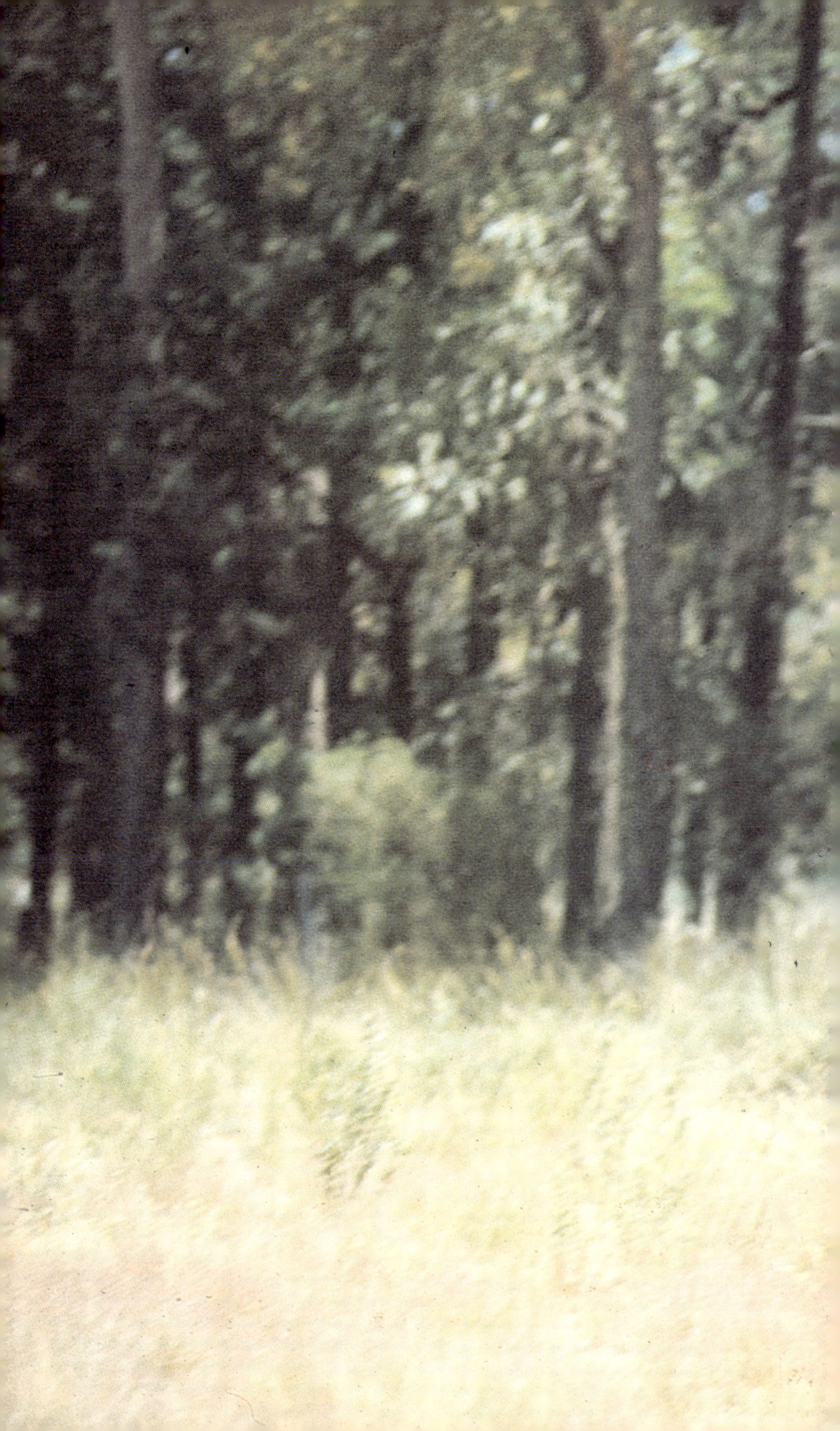

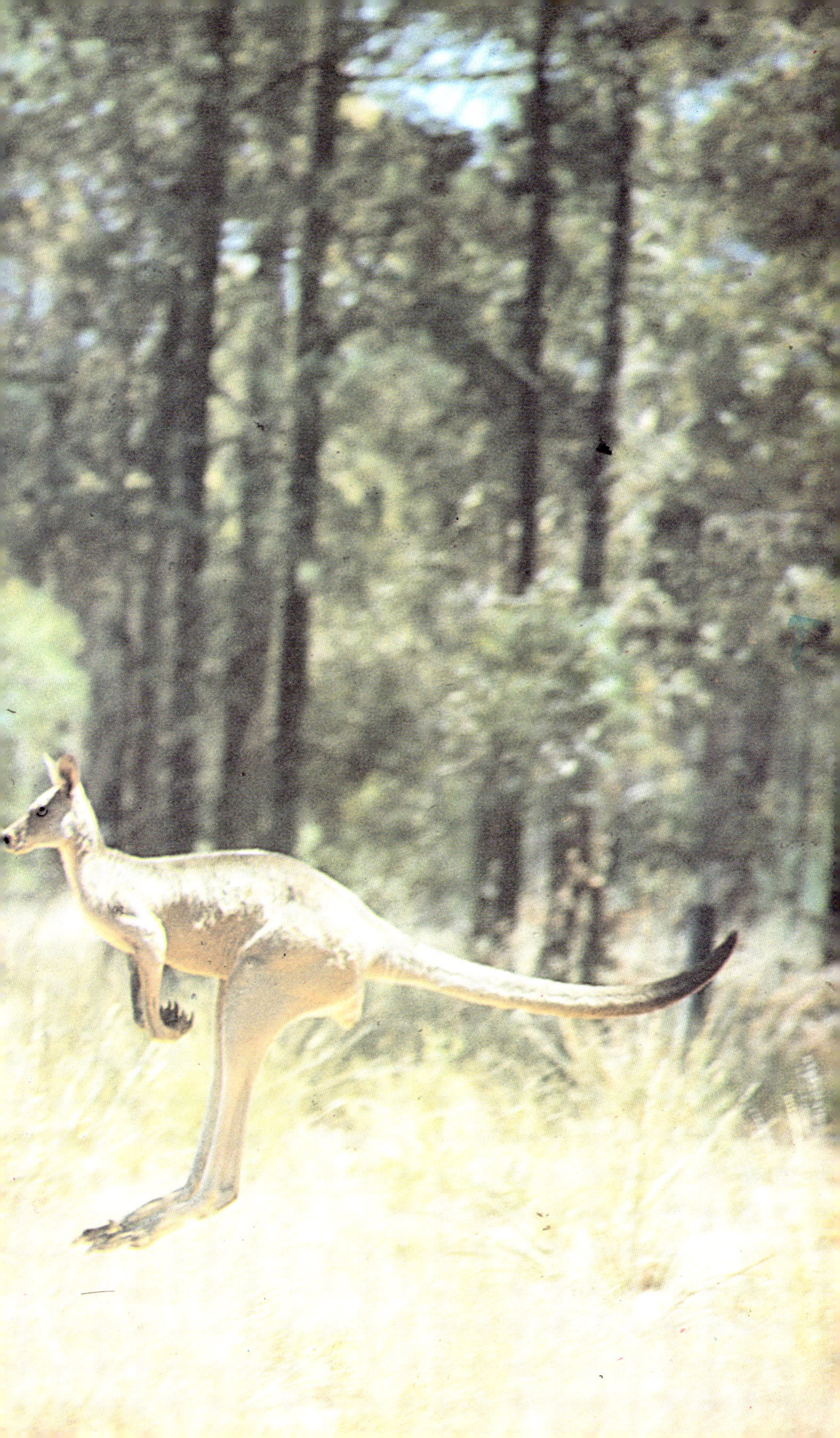